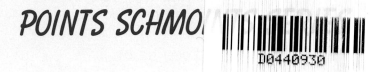

POINTS SCHMO

D0440930

Better Bidding Judgement
The Bergen Way

Understanding
1NT Forcing

Bergen Books

ACKNOWLEDGEMENTS

Layout, cover design, and editing by
Hammond Graphics.

My very special thanks to: Cheryl Bergen, Gary Blaiss,
Caitlin, Nancy Deal, Ned Downey, Pete Filandro,
Jim Garnher, Terry Gerber, Meredith Gunter,
Pat Harrington, Steve Jones, Al Kimel, Alex Martelli,
Harriet and Dave Morris, Jan Nathan,
Phyllis Nicholson, Dan Oakes, Mark Raphaelson,
Jesse Reisman, Jeff Rubens, Eric Sandberg,
Maggie Sparrow, Tom Spector, Merle Stetser,
and Bobby Stinebaugh.

Bergen Books
9 River Chase Terrace
Palm Beach Gardens, FL 33418-6817

Copyright 2002 © by Marty Bergen.
All rights reserved including the right of reproduction,
in whole or in part, in any form.
First Edition published 2002.
Printed in the United States of America.
10 9 8 7 6 5 4 3 2

First Printing: September, 2002
Second Printing: July, 2007

ISBN   0-9716636-3-7

♠ ♡ Caribbean Bridge Cruises ♢ ♣
with Marty Bergen and Larry Cohen

All cruises depart and return to Ft. Lauderdale, Florida
For prices, itinerary, flyers and other info, or to be on the mailing list
for future cruises with Marty and Larry, call:

Bruce Travel 1-800-367-9980

To participate in bridge activities,
you must book the cruise with Bruce Travel.

These cruises feature daily lectures, as much duplicate bridge as you
care to play, plus all the activities, entertainment and ambiance that
you'd expect to find on a first-class cruise ship.

2007 Cruise with Larry Cohen

Many-time National Champion and popular speaker/author.
Sunday, Nov 4 - Sunday, Nov 11. Ports include: St. Thomas,
Bahamas, Virgin Islands, Road Town Tortola, etc.

2008 Cruise with Marty Bergen

Renowned lecturer/teacher, author of 19 books and ten-time
National Champion Marty Bergen's next cruise will take place
Sunday Nov 16 - Sunday Nov 23, 2008. Ports include: Bahamas,
Mexico, Costa Maya, Grand Cayman, Turks & Caicos Islands, Half
Moon Cay, etc. Highlights include: daily lessons featuring brand-new
material with a dynamic approach.

• Free Bergen book for those signing up early •
• Free private lesson for groups of 5 signing up together •
• Free drawing to play duplicate on cruise with Marty •

For info on books and CDs
with GREAT DISCOUNTS,
please refer to pages 47-48.

To order, call **1-800-386-7432**
or email: mbergen@mindspring.com

Contents

Last, But Definitely Not Least

Stop – Read This

This outline will prove to be helpful in aiding your understanding and enjoyment of this book.

Pages 6-13, "First Things First" sets the scene with some essential details about 1NT Forcing.

Pages 14-31 form the heart of the book. Here you will find a thorough discussion of opener's and responder's rebids. **The two facing pages always go hand-in-hand.** The pages on the left illustrate and explain opener's rebids. The corresponding pages on the right address responder's rebid. Some examples are straightforward, while others are more challenging.

In this section, the suit opened may vary, as will opener's rebid. This allows the reader to experience many different auctions. However, for each pair of facing pages, the principles are identical.

Be aware that I treat a 5-card suit as a 1- point asset in notrump. You may not agree, but that explains why I don't open 1NT with 17 HCP and a 5-card suit (17 + 1 = 18), and why opener's 2NT rebid shows 17-18 HCP, not 18-19.

Pages 32-33 features auctions where opener jumps to game. Is that (or is that not) a shutout bid?

Pages 34-46, "Last, But Definitely Not Least," includes additional important information about 1NT Forcing: examples of well-bid and well-played hands, other topics of interest, and competitive bidding and partnership issues.

1NT Forcing Response to a Major
(Unpassed Hand, No Competition)

- Forcing for one round, does not promise a rebid
- 5-12 HCP (both 5 and 12 are rare)
- Denies a hand strong enough to force to game
- Balanced or unbalanced distribution
- Used when playing 2/1
- Denies 4-card support for opener's major
- 3-card support for opener's major *only* with a subminimum raise, or a limit raise
- A 1NT response to 1♡ denies four spades
- After a 1NT response, opener says "forcing"

Minimum strength for a 1NT response (after 1♠):

♠ 9   ♡ K 8 7 3   ♢ Q 9 3 2   ♣ 10 6 4 2
♠ J 7 4   ♡ Q 5 2   ♢ J 8 3   ♣ Q 10 5 4
♠ 8 4   ♡ A J 8 7 3 2   ♢ 8 6 5 2   ♣ 2

Maximum strength for a 1NT response (after 1♠):

♠ 6   ♡ K J 7 2   ♢ Q J 3 2   ♣ A J 6 4
♠ 3 2   ♡ A 5   ♢ K Q 8 6 5   ♣ Q 8 6 4

Comparing:	1NT Forcing	1NT Nonforcing
HCP range:	5 – terrible 12	6 – bad 10
support for major:	possible	never
distribution:	anything	anything

Answering Frequently Asked Questions

1. "Is 1NT Forcing a radical change from "Standard?"
Marty Sez: No. Responder usually has the same weak hand (6-10 HCP) as if 1NT were nonforcing.

2. "When playing 1NT Forcing, what do you give up?"
Marty Sez: You can no longer stop in 1NT. If that was the best contract for your side, *c'est la vie.*

3. "When is this convention necessary?"
Marty Sez: Playing 2/1 Game-Forcing, a 2-level response in a new suit is forcing to game. Most invitational hands (11-ish HCP) are not strong enough for the 2/1 bid, but are too strong for a traditional 1NT response. Without 1NT Forcing, invitational hands would be unbiddable.

4. "What if I play 1NT Forcing, but don't play 2/1?"
Marty Sez: I don't recommend this. 1NT Forcing should support 2/1 by handling invitational hands. If not playing 2/1, invitational hands *are* strong enough for the two level.

5. "Is there more than one way to play 2/1?"
Marty Sez: Yes. Playing 2/1 Game-Forcing, you *always* go to game. Other 2/1 players make one exception: if responder later rebids his suit, opener can pass with a minimum hand. I prefer the "always" approach; in any relationship, I want to know exactly where I stand.

In conclusion, **Marty Sez:** More and more players are using 1NT Forcing. Even if you don't play it, you can be sure that many of your opponents will. Learning more about it is a must.

If You Don't (Always) Open 1NT with a 5-Card Major

What do you open with a balanced hand (5-3-3-2), a 5-card major, and the strength to open 1NT? Probably no other bridge topic results in such contrasting opinions and strong-willed points of view.

I have heard all of the following many times:
1. "I always ignore the major and open 1NT."
2. "I never open 1NT with a 5-card major."
3. "I open 1NT with 5 hearts, but not with 5 spades."
4. "I open 1NT with a weak suit, but not a strong suit."
5. "I open my major unless all suits are stopped."
6. "I open 1NT if I have three cards in the other major."

Any book on 1NT Forcing must naturally address opener's rebids. Authorities agree that a 5-3-3-2 hand with 15-16 HCP is not strong enough to raise a 1NT response to 2NT. Therefore, if you open a major and partner responds 1NT, you should now bid your cheapest 3-card minor. However, you'll note that there are NO examples in this book where opener rebids 2♣ or 2♦ with a hand that could have opened 1NT. Why is that?

I certainly have no idea which of the above approaches is the most popular. I also must confess that I totally believe in approach #1. Therefore, if I would ALWAYS open 1NT with:

♠ A Q 7 5 3   ♡ A Q 8   ♦ 6 3 2   ♣ K 10
I can't (in good conscience) recommend that you open 1♠ and rebid 2♦ after partner responds 1NT Forcing.

Does She or Doesn't She Have a Real Suit?

If opener has no good rebid, but can't pass 1NT *Forcing*, she bids a 3-card minor. No one likes it, but it goes with the territory. Responder needs 5-card support to be happy. If opener bids a 3-card suit, and responder has to pass with four cards, life goes on. But if responder passes with only three cards, you'd be in a 3-3 "fit" — no thank you.

It would definitely be helpful if responder could know how likely opener is to have a 3-card minor. And she can!

With 3-3 in the minors and a balanced minimum, opener always rebids 2♣. **Therefore, opener's 2♣ rebid is more likely to be a 3-card suit than 2♦.** (This is the same as opener's mindset when she needs to open a 3-card minor.)

With five spades, four hearts and a minimum opening bid, partner opens 1♠ and then painlessly bids 2♡. But if she has four spades and five hearts, she needs 17 HCP to *reverse* into spades. When her minimum opening bid includes four spades, five hearts, and a 3-card minor, she will bid her minor. Therefore, **opener is more likely to bid a 3-card minor after opening 1♡ than 1♠.**

Is opener likely to bid a 3-card minor after 1NT?

1♡ - 1NT		1♠ - 1NT	
2♣ is most likely.		2♦ is least likely.	

1♡ - 1NT	*and*	1♠ - 1NT	
2♦		2♣ fall in-between.	

By the way: Players who open 1NT with a 5-card major are much less likely to need to bid a 3-card minor.

Relevant Bidding Style for This Book

Our Opening Bids

We open light, based on The Rule of 20. In first and second seat, add the length of your two longest suits to your HCP. If the total is 20 (or more), open the bidding, unless the hand has serious flaws.

We do open 1NT with a 5-card major and a balanced hand.

With five hearts, four spades, and an opening bid, we always open 1♡ (we're not playing Flannery 2♢).

After Partner Opens a Major and RHO Passes:

A 1NT response is forcing by an unpassed hand.

Responder's new suit at the two level is forcing to game. (2/1 Game-Forcing)

A single raise is "semi-constructive." This means that responder's immediate raise to two will never be based on a "lousy" 6-point hand. If he does have a "garbage raise," he responds 1NT, and then takes a preference to opener's major suit.

An immediate limit raise requires four trumps.

By the way: If partner opens a minor, a 1NT response is definitely *not* forcing.

Opener Rebids After 1♠ – 1NT

The only forcing bid is a jump-shift.

Rebid	Likely Length	Probable HCP
2♣, 2♢	3+ cards	at most 18
2♡	4 hearts	at most 18
2♠	6 spades	at most 15
2NT	5-3-3-2	17-18
3♣, 3♢	4 cards	19+
3♡	4 hearts	19+
3♠	6 spades	16-17
3NT	5-3-3-2	19
4♠	7 spades 8 spades	14+ 12+

After 1♡ – 1NT, all concepts are identical.
In addition:

2♠ reverse	4 spades	17+

Responder's Rebids
(After Opener Rebids 2 of a Minor)

Pass shows: 5-8 HCP with no good bid.

Preference to opener's major shows:
    A doubleton with less than 11 HCP.   OR
    A very weak 3-card raise (much less often).

2NT shows:
    10-12 HCP.
    No fit for opener's major.
    Stoppers in unbid suits.

Raising opener's minor shows:
    5-card support, usually.
    At least 10 points, including distribution.

Jump raise in opener's major shows:
    3-card limit raise.
    11-ish (good 10 to a bad 12) distribution points.

New Suit:

2 level: 5-9 HCP, and a six-card suit.
        (A strong 5-card suit is possible.)

3 level (nonjump):
    A good 6-card suit with 5-11 HCP.

3 level (jump):
    A very good 6-card suit with 10-11 HCP.

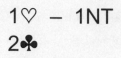

1♡ – 1NT
2♣

Opener's likely length in hearts and clubs:
5-4, 5-3, 5-5, 6-4

Worth knowing: This is the most likely auction for opener to bid a 3-card suit at his second turn.

Examples of 2♣ rebids:

♠ K 9   ♡ A J 5 3 2   ◇ K J 7   ♣ 4 3 2
Nice clubs! Oh well.

♠ Q 9 6 5   ♡ A K 8 5 3   ◇ 8   ♣ A Q 3
You're not strong enough to reverse.

♠ Q   ♡ A Q 7 6 4   ◇ A K J   ♣ Q 7 5 3
Not strong enough to jump-shift, and bidding notrump with a singleton spade is premature. Responder will rarely pass 2♣.

♠ A 6   ♡ A 9 7 6 4 3   ◇ 8   ♣ A Q 10 4
Your strong clubs, weak hearts, and nice hand all argue for 2♣ rather than 2♡.

♠ A K J 2   ♡ J 8 6 4 3   ◇ 8 5   ♣ K 9
Yuck! No rational alternative. For your information, after 1NT Forcing, if opener occasionally has to bid a 2-card minor, no alert is required.

Responder Rebids After 1♠ – 1NT
2♣ – ???

Pass with: ♠ J   ♡ K 7 5 3   ◇ J 9 6 3   ♣ Q 8 7 2

Bid 2◇ with: ♠ 9   ♡ K 6 4   ◇ Q J 9 7 4 3   ♣ 9 4 2

2♡ with: ♠ 6 4   ♡ K J 10 8 5 4   ◇ K 6 5 2   ♣ 9

2♠ with: ♠ Q 8   ♡ J 6 4 3   ◇ K J 4 3   ♣ J 7 6

2♠ with: ♠ 8 6 5   ♡ Q 9 6 4   ◇ J 7 4   ♣ Q J 10

2NT with: ♠ J 4   ♡ K Q 9 8   ◇ K J 8 7   ♣ J 8 4

3♣ with: ♠ 8   ♡ A J 7   ◇ 8 6 5 4   ♣ K J 8 7 5

3◇ with: ♠ 7 6   ♡ 8 6 5   ◇ K Q J 9 6 4   ♣ A 4
If you're not playing 2/1 as 100% game-forcing, you would have responded 2◇ and then rebid 3◇ (invitational).

3♡ with: ♠ A   ♡ Q J 10 7 5 2   ◇ K 4 2   ♣ 9 8 6
Similar to the jump to 3◇.

3♠ with: ♠ A 8 6   ♡ K 6   ◇ K J 5 3   ♣ 7 6 4 2

4♣ with: ♠ 7   ♡ A 10 7 6 2   ◇ 9   ♣ Q J 10 7 6 4
Promising 6-card support and great shape.

4♠ with: ♠ Q 9 4   ♡ 7 5   ◇ A 7 2   ♣ K J 10 9 2
Based on your great club fit.

1♡ – 1NT
2◇

Opener's likely length in hearts and diamonds:
5-4, 5-3, 5-5, 6-4

Keep in mind: A 3◇ jump-shift would be game-forcing, so opener can rebid 2◇ with a very good hand.

Examples of 2◇ rebids:

♠ — ♡ K J 8 6 5 ◇ A Q 9 7 ♣ Q 6 5 3
With two 4-card minors, you might as well bid your stronger suit.

♠ A Q 7 ♡ A 8 6 5 4 2 ◇ A Q 10 ♣ 9
The hearts are not good enough for 3♡, and the hand is too good to rebid 2♡. The temporizing rebid of 2◇ is best. If partner has a weak hand with four diamonds and one heart and passes 2◇, that's okay.

Don't rebid 2◇ with:

♠ K Q 6 ♡ A K J 7 5 ◇ A 10 8 ♣ 5 3
Bid 2NT. You have the right strength and distribution for this bid, and you can't worry about your weak clubs. **Only bid a 3-card suit when you must.**

♠ Q 7 5 ♡ A K Q J 4 ◇ 10 9 7 ♣ 6 2
Bid 2♡. Feels like a 6-card suit to me.

Responder Rebids After 1♠ – 1NT
2◇ – ???

♠ 6 ♡ Q 8 6 4 2 ◇ K 8 4 ♣ Q 7 6 4

Pass. If you're considering a rescue bid of 2♡, don't. When partner opens 1♠, and rebids 2◇, a 3-card suit is rare.

♠ 7 ♡ K Q J 9 6 ◇ 6 4 ♣ 9 6 5 4 2

Bid 2♡. Looks like a 6-card suit, not that you have any better options.

♠ 3 2 ♡ A 8 6 4 3 ◇ 7 4 ♣ A 7 5 4

Bid 2♠. Your spades are lousy, and opener could easily have three hearts. However, if partner has a singleton heart, it could be disastrous to bid hearts with only five. **After a 1♠ opening bid, finding a heart fit is never easy.**

♠ K J ♡ 8 6 5 ◇ J 7 5 3 ♣ A 7 5 2

Bid 2♠. A sensible compromise between 3◇ and pass.

♠ 9 ♡ 8 6 4 ◇ K Q 4 2 ♣ A Q 7 4 3

Bid 3◇. No one enjoys raising a potential 3-card suit to the three level with four trumps. Fortunately, partner is not likely to have a 3-card diamond suit on *this* auction. Regardless, all other actions are unthinkable.

1♠ – 1NT
2♡

Opener's likely length in spades and hearts:
5-4, 5-5, 6-4

Examples of 2♡ rebids:

♠ A Q 7 5 3   ♡ K J 7 4   ◇ A   ♣ Q J 3
Not strong enough for a 3♡ jump-shift, which forces a potentially weak responder to game.

♠ K J 10 7 4   ♡ A Q 9 6 2   ◇ 6 3   ♣ 4
I hope that you would open with this classic Rule of 20 hand, despite having "only 10 HCP."

♠ K Q 6 5 4 2   ♡ A K Q 7   ◇ 9 7   ♣ 4
With 6-4 distribution and a nonminimum hand, it's usually correct to show the 4-card suit at your second turn.

Don't rebid 2♡ with:

♠ K Q J 9 7 5   ♡ A 7 5 3   ◇ Q 5   ♣ 7
You have great spades, moderate hearts and a minimum opening bid, so 2♠ is a standout.

♠ A K 10 9 7   ♡ A K J 10 8   ◇ 8 5 4   ♣ —
Bid 3♡. One doesn't usually jump-shift with 15 HCP. But if you rebid 2♡ and everyone passed, you'd be very nervous before seeing partner's hand. You need very little help to make a major-suit game.

Responder Rebids After 1♠ - 1NT
2♡ - ???

♠ 7   ♡ 8 6 3   ◇ K 8 6 4   ♣ K 8 5 4 2
Pass. Not fun, but it could have been worse.
What if your ♡3 had been the ◇3?

♠ J 6   ♡ J 6 5   ◇ J 7 4 3 2   ♣ K 5 4
Pass. With this garbage, don't give opener a chance to
bid again.

♠ J 6   ♡ J 6 5   ◇ A K 10 9 2   ♣ 5 4 2
Bid 2♠. The normal action with three hearts and two
spades. **A 5-2 trump suit is usually better than a 4 -3.**

♠ K 3   ♡ 9 6   ◇ A 10 8 7   ♣ Q J 8 6 4
Bid 2NT to invite game.

♠ 8   ♡ K 7 4   ◇ A Q 10 9 7 5   ♣ 7 4 3
Bid 3◇. Game is still possible, so you shouldn't pass,
especially given your lovely diamond suit.

♠ 6 4   ♡ K Q 10 4   ◇ K 9 8 5   ♣ 7 4 3
Bid 3♡. Support with support.

♠ K J 9   ♡ 7 5   ◇ 9 6 5 3   ♣ A Q 8 6
Bid 3♠. A textbook example of a delayed limit raise.

♠ 5   ♡ K 8 6 3 2   ◇ 7 4   ♣ A 10 9 5 3
Bid 4♡. Too much offense to bid only 3♡.

1♡ – 1NT
2♡

Opener's likely length in his suit:
Six cards, because many hands with a 7-card suit are worth
a jump to 3♡.

Worth knowing: Opener's strength is more limited when
he rebids his suit than for any other rebid. If he has more
than a minimum opening bid with a strong suit, he can
make an invitational jump to three.

Examples of 2♡ rebids:

♠ K J 8   ♡ K J 6 4 3 2   ◇ K Q   ♣ K 4
Despite the 16 HCP, your weak suit and aceless hand
suggest taking the low road.

♠ A K 8 6   ♡ K Q J 9 7   ◇ 8 5   ♣ 6 4
A very rare example of rebidding a 5-card suit after 1NT.
What else can you do?

Don't rebid 2♡ with:

♠ 9   ♡ A K Q J 9 7   ◇ A 9 8   ♣ 8 6 4
Bid 3♡. With the solid suit and seven sure tricks, you
should jump, even though you have only 14 HCP.

♠ 6 3   ♡ A J 9 6 4 3   ◇ 8   ♣ A K J 6
2♣ is far more flexible. Most nice 6-4 hands should show
their second suit.

Responder Rebids After 1♠ – 1NT
2♠ – ???

♠ 7 ♡ K 8 7 ◇ K J 8 6 3 ♣ Q J 5 4
Pass. You have a misfit for opener's suit, and his 2♠ rebid limited his hand.

♠ — ♡ J 8 5 ◇ K 8 6 5 4 2 ♣ K 7 5 4
Pass. Diamonds may be a better combined trump suit than spades — then again, it might not. No double, no trouble.

♠ J 6 ♡ A Q 4 ◇ J 10 9 3 ♣ Q J 8 3
Bid 2NT. A rare example of a 1NT Forcing hand that should bid 2NT after opener rebids a 6-card major. Most hands either pass or raise the major.

♠ 7 ♡ Q J 10 3 ◇ 5 4 ♣ K Q J 10 7 4
Bid 3♣. You need a suit like this to overrule partner's 6-card major.

♠ A 7 ♡ 5 3 ◇ A J 10 8 4 ♣ 7 4 3 2
Bid 3♠. With an 8-card fit, two aces, a nice source of tricks, and a potential ruffing value, game is very possible.

♠ J 10 5 ♡ 8 7 5 ◇ 8 ♣ A K 10 9 8 6
Bid 4♠. Once opener promises six spades, you must insist on game with this promising hand.

1♥ - 1NT
2♠

Opener's likely length in hearts and spades:
5-4, 6-4

Keep in mind: The 2♠ reverse shows 17 HCP and is forcing for one round.

Worth knowing: Because responder denies four spades, opener might decide to ignore his spade suit.

Examples of 2♠ rebids:

♠ A K J 9   ♥ A K J 10 6   ♦ 7 5 3   ♣ 6
With all your honors concentrated in your two long suits, you are worth a reverse despite having "only" 16 HCP.

♠ K Q 9 7 5   ♥ A 10 9 8 4 3   ♦ —   ♣ A 7
On those rare occasions when you do have 6-5, come alive. This is definitely a "Points Schmoints" hand. You plan to rebid 3♠ to show five spades and therefore six hearts (you would have opened 1♠ with 5-5).

Don't rebid 2♠ with:

♠ K J 7 5   ♥ A Q 8 6 4   ♦ A J   ♣ K Q
Bid 3NT. With such strong doubletons, you can afford to be direct.

♠ A 6 4 3   ♥ A K Q 10 7 5   ♦ J 4   ♣ K
Bid 3♥. No reason to avoid this descriptive rebid.

Responder Rebids After 1♡ – 1NT
2♠ – ???

Keep in mind: Opener's reverse is forcing, but not necessarily to game.

Worth knowing: If responder bids 2NT or 3♡, opener can pass. However, if responder bids a new suit, that should be forcing to game.

♠752 ♡43 ◇Q964 ♣KJ42
Bid 2NT.

♠A84 ♡104 ◇AJ9753 ♣53
Bid 3◇, exploring for the best game.

♠J86 ♡K7 ◇K7642 ♣754
Bid 3♡, taking a preference to opener's 5-card suit.

♠AQ10 ♡J ◇7632 ♣98653
Bid 3♠. Because 1NT denied four spades, partner will know that you have three good ones.

♠753 ♡84 ◇KQ96 ♣AJ64
Bid 3NT.

♠K7 ♡432 ◇K109653 ♣K2
Bid 4♡. Your hearts may not be pretty, but show your 3-card limit raise with a jump.

1♥ - 1NT
2NT

Opener's likely hand-type:
A balanced hand with 17-18 HCP

Keep in mind: On this auction, expect a spade lead, because the opponents usually lead the unbid major.

Examples of 2NT rebids:

♠ K J 6 ♥ K Q 8 5 4 ◇ Q J 2 ♣ A Q
A classic example of opener's invitational 2NT rebid.

♠ K 9 5 4 ♥ A J 8 6 3 ◇ A J ♣ K Q
The invitational raise to 2NT does a better job of limiting your hand than 2♠. Remember, partner's 1NT response denied four spades.

Don't rebid 2NT with:

♠ A 8 7 ♥ A Q J 10 5 ◇ A K ♣ 8 6 4
Bid 3NT. With an "excellent 18-count," don't risk being dropped in a part score.

♠ 7 4 ♥ A K 6 4 2 ◇ K Q 7 ♣ K Q J
Bid 2♣, only. You are very concerned about a spade lead in notrump. Remember, 1♥ – 1NT denies four spades.

By the way: Opinions vary as to the exact number of HCP opener needs to raise 1NT to 2NT. It is worth discussing with your partner.

Responder Rebids After 1♠ – 1NT
2NT – ???

Keep in mind: Although 2NT is not forcing, responder should rarely pass once opener shows 17-18 HCP.

Worth knowing: Should responder's new suit be forcing on this auction? I play it that way.

♠ 7 5   ♡ 8 6 4 3   ◇ K Q 8   ♣ J 5 4 2
Pass. With only 6 HCP, you have no reason to accept opener's invitation.

♠ K 10   ♡ 9   ◇ J 9 7 5   ♣ K Q 8 6 5 3
Bid 3♣. You might belong in 3NT, but you also might belong in 5♣, 6♣, or even 4♠.

♠ 8 6   ♡ K J 9 7 6   ◇ A J 6 4   ♣ 7 4
Bid 3♡, on your way to 4♡ or 3NT.

♠ 9 6 4   ♡ 8 5   ◇ Q 10 6 2   ♣ K 9 5 3
Bid 3♠, signing off with the very weak raise.

♠ 9 7   ♡ J 7   ◇ A K Q 9 7   ♣ 8 6 4 3
Bid 3NT. As usual, forget about five of a minor.

♠ Q 9 5   ♡ J 8 6 5 3   ◇ A 7   ♣ K 5 2
Bid 4♠. Rely on the 8-card fit in opener's major.

1♠ – 1NT
3♣

Opener's likely length in spades and clubs:
5-4, 6-4, 5-5, 6-3

Keep in mind: Opener needs 19 HCP, or a strong hand with great shape, for the game-forcing jump-shift.

Examples of 3♣ rebids:

♠ A Q J 9 6 ♡ A 4 ◇ 7 ♣ K Q J 10 4
Only 17 HCP, but, with your tremendous playing strength, you have enough to jump-shift.

♠ A K J 8 5 ♡ A ◇ A K 7 ♣ 10 6 5 3
No one enjoys bidding such a bad suit on a possible slam hand, but the alternatives are all unattractive.

♠ A K 7 5 4 2 ♡ A J 6 ◇ 4 ♣ A K 9
You must force to game, so the "white lie" about your club length is necessary. Responder should be reluctant to raise your minor suit on these auctions.

Don't rebid 3♣ with:

♠ K Q 8 7 2 ♡ K Q ◇ K J ♣ A Q 8 5
Bid 3NT. You're not interested in playing in 5♣.
With your strong doubletons, a simple 3NT is best.

Responder Rebids After 1♡ – 1NT
3♢ – ???

♠ J 6 4   ♡ J 3   ♢ A 7 5   ♣ 9 6 5 3 2
Bid 3♡. This preference is usually based on a doubleton.

♠ Q 4   ♡ J 3   ♢ J 8 6 3 2   ♣ Q 6 5 3
Bid 3♡. With a hand that lacks slam interest, ignore your five-card support for partner's minor suit and support his major suit. If opener has good hearts, 10 tricks in hearts are more likely than 11 tricks in diamonds.

♠ K Q 10   ♡ J 3   ♢ 8 6 4   ♣ Q J 8 6 4
Bid 3NT. With such good black cards, you don't need to show your doubleton heart.

♠ 7 5   ♡ A 3   ♢ K Q 10 6 2   ♣ 9 8 6 5
Bid 4♢. With this hand, 6♢ is looking good.

♠ 7 5   ♡ 3   ♢ K Q 10 6 2   ♣ J 9 8 6 5
Bid 5♢. Because a raise to 4♢ would be forcing, you try to avoid unnecessary jumps to the five level. The only justification for this "fast arrival" bid is that you want to show:

> great trump support (5+ cards with strength),
> no interest in opener's major,
> a minimum hand, with no aces.

Why, specifically, zero aces? If partner is interested in slam, he must know the ace situation once you have deprived him of the ability to bid Blackwood.

Opener's likely length in spades and hearts:
5-4, 5-5, 6-4

Worth knowing: When opener has great length in the majors, he can jump-shift even if he is a touch "light."

Examples of 3♡ rebids:

♠ A Q 10 6 2   ♡ A K J 9   ◇ A J 8   ♣ 2
You expect to make game in spades, hearts, or notrump.

♠ A 9 7 6 4 3 2   ♡ A K Q 7   ◇ A   ♣ 9
If partner responds 3NT, rebid 4♠.

♠ A K Q 6 5   ♡ A 10 9 4   ◇ K Q 9 6   ♣ —
If responder bids 3♠ or 3NT, you will then bid 4◇.

Don't rebid 3♡ with:

♠ A K Q J 10 4   ♡ Q 6 5 3   ◇ Q J   ♣ A
Bid a practical 4♠. It's possible that you belong in a partscore, or a slam, or a heart contract. However, all of these are unlikely.

♠ K Q 7 5 4   ♡ A J 6 3   ◇ Q J   ♣ K Q
With this awful 18-count, you're not worth a game-forcing jump-shift.

Responder Rebids After 1♠ – 1NT
3♥ – ???

♠ A 5 ♥ Q 7 6 ◇ 9 6 5 ♣ 8 6 5 4 2
Bid 3♠. Avoid raising partner's second suit with only three cards. If opener has 5-5 in the majors, he will rebid 4♥, and you will happily pass.

♠ J 6 3 ♥ Q 7 ◇ Q 7 6 4 3 2 ♣ J 4
Bid 3♠. If opener rebids 3NT, you will bid 4♠.

♠ 9 ♥ J 6 3 ◇ K J 9 6 ♣ Q 10 8 6 4
Bid 3NT. Nice and easy.

♠ K ♥ 7 4 2 ◇ K Q 9 7 6 5 3 ♣ 7 2
Bid 4◇, showing your long suit and awaiting opener's next move. However, be careful. After 1NT Forcing, some experienced players (not I) treat responder's new suit at the four level as artificial.

♠ 9 ♥ Q 9 7 6 ◇ K 8 6 5 3 2 ♣ Q 7
Bid 4♥. Happy as can be.

♠ 8 ♥ K Q 8 ◇ Q 6 5 4 3 ♣ 7 6 5 3
Bid 4♥. Not happy, but nothing else is appealing.

♠ Q 5 3 ♥ K 10 5 ◇ A 8 6 ♣ Q 9 5 3
Bid 4♠. This promises a 3-card limit raise. If that's all opener needs for slam, he's welcome to bid on.

1♠ – 1NT
3♠

Opener's likely length in spades:
Usually six cards, sometimes seven.

Worth knowing: Opener typically has 16 -17 HCP for the invitational jump, but HCP alone are not the key. He needs a long, strong suit with extra values, but not enough strength to force to game.

Examples of 3♠ rebids:

♠ K Q J 10 5 2   ♡ A Q   ◇ K 9 8   ♣ 3 2
Look at that beautiful suit. Not a bad hand, either.

♠ A K Q 9 7 6 3   ♡ 6   ◇ 8 3   ♣ K 7 4
When you have a great 7-card suit, you don't need a lot of HCP to jump.

Don't rebid 3♠ with:

♠ A K 10 7 5 3   ♡ A 4   ◇ A Q 9 8   ♣ 6
Bid 3◇. You are strong enough to insist on game.

♠ K 8 6 4 3 2   ♡ Q 6 3   ◇ K J   ♣ A K
Bid 2♠. Don't jump with such a weak spade suit.

♠ Q J 10 9 8 5 3   ♡ A   ◇ K Q J 10   ♣ 6
Bid 4♠. With spades as trump, you have nine playing tricks. All you need from partner is the ♠K or any ace.

Responder Rebids After 1♡ – 1NT
3♡ – ???

Keep in mind: When opener jumps in his major suit, responder should not get too imaginative. He should usually either raise to 4♡, or pass.

♠ 9 6 5   ♡ 4 2   ◇ Q 8 7 5 4   ♣ K J 6
Pass. Having support for partner's six-card suit is a plus, but having only 6 HCP is a bigger minus.

♠ 9 7 6   ♡ —   ◇ K 9 8 6 5 3   ♣ A J 5 3
Pass. Although you're not a happy camper, you should bite the bullet. You're not likely to make a game contract. **When the hand is a misfit, stop bidding ASAP.**

♠ K Q 9   ♡ 8   ◇ Q 7 5 3 2   ♣ A 9 6 4
Bid 3NT. The heart singleton is a liability, but you have too much to pass.

♠ 8 6   ♡ 2   ◇ K Q 2   ♣ A J 8 6 5 3 2
Bid 4♣. You hope that you have a game somewhere.

♠ Q 10 6   ♡ A 6 3   ◇ 8 7   ♣ K J 9 6 5
Bid 4♡. Once opener doesn't force to game, don't even think about slam.

♠ A 8 5   ♡ Q   ◇ 8 6 5 3   ♣ K 8 7 4 2
Bid 4♡. When partner promises a 6-card suit, you can support him with a singleton honor.

1♠ – 1NT
3NT

Opener's likely hand-type: A strong, balanced hand with 19-20 HCP, where opening 2NT was possible.

Examples of 3NT rebids:

♠ A K 9 7 3   ♡ 8 4   ◇ K Q J   ♣ A Q 7

♠ A K Q 8 5   ♡ K Q   ◇ 8 6 4 3   ♣ K Q

Jumping in notrump is more practical than jump-shifting in diamonds.

Responder Rebids After 1♠ – 1NT
3NT – ???

♠ 8 3   ♡ K Q 7 5 3   ◇ K J 5   ♣ Q 6 3

Pass. Don't bother looking for hearts or slam.

♠ K 6   ♡ 6   ◇ A Q J 8 5 3   ♣ 9 6 4 3

Bid 4◇. Definitely worth investigating a diamond slam.

♠ A 7   ♡ Q 9 8 7 5 3   ◇ 8 5   ♣ 10 7 4

Bid 4♡. Obvious, once opener promises 2-3 hearts.

♠ 6 4 2   ♡ Q 4   ◇ K 9 6 3 2   ♣ 10 5 4

Bid 4♠. You hope you were right to not pass 1♠.

♠ J 8 6   ♡ A 10 9 3   ◇ 8 6   ♣ A 10 6 4

Bid 4♠. Opposite a balanced 19-20, slam is unlikely.

1♡ - 1NT
4♡

Opener promises: A long suit; either a moderate eight, a good seven, or even a great six. He also needs a hand strong enough to justify game even if responder has only six points. Other than being too strong to open four of his major, and not strong enough to open 2♣, opener's strength is not well-defined.

Examples of 4♡ rebids:

♠ 9 7   ♡ K Q J 8 7 5 4 2   ◇ —   ♣ A Q 6

♠ 7 4 3   ♡ A K J 10 9 7 6 4   ◇ 5   ♣ A

♠ K Q   ♡ K Q J 7 6 4 3   ◇ K Q 5   ♣ 5

♠ A Q 9 6   ♡ Q J 10 9 7 5 3   ◇ K J   ♣ —

♠ A K 5   ♡ A Q J 10 9 4   ◇ Q J 9   ♣ 2

Responder Rebids After 1♡ – 1NT
4♡ – ???

Because opener did not promise a lot of HCP, responder should usually pass. The only exception would be a maximum hand with exceptional controls, perhaps:

♠ 7   ♡ A 8   ◇ A Q 10 9 2   ♣ 9 7 6 5 4
(With this hand, I would bid 4NT.)

An Elegant Trump Coup

Contract: 4♡
Lead: ♠Q

North
♠ 7 6 4
♡ 3
♢ A 10 5 4
♣ A 9 8 6 2

West
♠ Q J 9 2
♡ —
♢ J 8 7 3 2
♣ K 7 5 3

East
♠ K 5 3
♡ 10 8 7 6 5
♢ K Q
♣ Q 10 4

South
♠ A 10 8
♡ A K Q J 9 4 2
♢ 9 6
♣ J

South	West	North	East
1♡	Pass	1NT	Pass
4♡	All Pass		

South won the ♠A and began drawing trumps, intending
to take his 10 easy tricks. The bad trump split was a shock.
However, once he regained his composure, he cashed two
more trumps, led the ♣J to the ♣A, and ruffed a club.
A diamond lead to the ace allowed a second club ruff.
South exited with the loser of his choice, and was then
sitting pretty with his ♡J 9 over East's ♡10 8.
Making four.

Well-Bid Hands

West	West	East	East
♠ K 8 7 6 4	1♠	1NT	♠ 10 9 2
♡ K Q 5 3	2♡	2♠	♡ 6 4 2
♢ 2	Pass		♢ Q J 6
♣ A K 8			♣ Q J 6 2

With 6 HCP, East had to respond, but was unwilling to encourage partner by raising spades immediately. His 1NT bid was a sensible compromise between pass and 2♠. West then showed his second suit, and East bid the obvious 2♠. After East's preference, West expected his partner to have a weak hand with two spades. Therefore, he called it a day. 2♠ was high enough.

West	West	East	East
♠ A Q 10 9 7 5	1♠	1NT	♠ —
♡ 8 5 2	2♠	Pass	♡ A K 6 3
♢ A			♢ J 7 6 3 2
♣ Q 8 3			♣ K 7 5 2

West's 2♠ rebid was not what East was hoping for. However, because of the misfit, he wisely refrained from further action. 2♠ was not an elegant contract, but West emerged with eight tricks: two hearts, one diamond, one club, and four spade winners.

West	West	East	East
♠ A J	1♡	1NT	♠ K 7 3
♡ A Q 7 5 3	2◇	2♡	♡ 10 6
◇ K Q 6 4 2	3◇	Pass	◇ J 7 5
♣ 8			♣ K 9 7 4 3

West had a very nice hand, but was not strong enough for a game-forcing jump-shift. After the 2◇ bid, East took a normal preference back to opener's five-card major suit. West was still interested in game, and rebid his diamonds. However, East was not tempted, and preferred to play in the known eight-card fit.

West	West	East	East
♠ 7 3	1♡	1NT	♠ Q J 9
♡ A K 8 6 4	2♣	3♣	♡ Q
◇ A 6	3◇	3NT	◇ 8 7 5 2
♣ K Q 9 2	Pass		♣ A 10 8 7 3

The first four bids were routine. Once East raised to 3♣, West was worth another bid. With no stopper in the unbid major, he was unwilling to barge into 3NT. His 3◇ bid promised something in that suit, which enabled East to bid the unbeatable 3NT.

Well-Bid Hands...continued

West		West	East		East	
♠ 9 8		1♡	1NT		♠ 7 5 3	
♡ A 8 6 4 3		2♣	4♡		♡ K Q 9	
◇ A 7 2		Pass			◇ 6 5	
♣ A 9 5					♣ K Q 8 6 4	

East intended to invite game with his 3-card limit raise. However, once opener bid clubs, East's magnificent fit for both suits persuaded him to go all the way. With normal splits, 11 tricks were easy.

West		West	East		East	
♠ 10 7 5 3 2		1♠	1NT		♠ 9	
♡ J		2◇	4◇		♡ A 8 5 3	
◇ A J 9 4		5◇	Pass		◇ K 10 8 7 5 2	
♣ A Q 3					♣ J 3	

East's modest hand really came to life when West bid 2◇. Raising to 3◇ would certainly not do justice to East's 6-card support, so he took the bull by the horns and jumped to 4◇.

West had no thoughts of game after the 1NT response, but took a second look at his hand after partner jumped. East had to have great shape and very long diamonds. West loved his holdings in hearts and clubs, and was no longer concerned about his weak spades. A very nice minor-suit game on 20 HCP.

1NT Semi-Forcing – An Alternate Approach

Some players (myself included) *love* 2/1 Game-Forcing, so we play 1NT Forcing. But if we open 1♠ and partner bids 1NT, we *hate* to bid 2♢ with a hand like this:

♠ J 7 6 4 3   ♡ K J 2   ♢ 4 3 2   ♣ A K

Therefore, we define (and announce) a 1NT response as "Semi-Forcing." Advocates of this style **pass** 1NT with minimum, balanced hands (such as the one above), that have no interest in game. Why?

- Your diamond suit is "nonexistent."
- If partner has a moderate hand, making seven tricks will be very difficult. Why bid higher?
- Partner will often take a preference to your major suit with a doubleton. Who needs that?
- Even if responder has a 3-card limit raise, a modest 1NT will be a better contract than THREE spades.
- If you play 1NT Semi-Forcing, you will need to bid a 3-card suit less often. That can't be bad.

1NT Semi-Forcing is not very different from 1NT Forcing. "Semi-Forcing" players respond 1NT with the same hands as their "Forcing" counterparts. However, with a shapely 3-card limit raise which can't stand to be dropped in 1NT, they make an immediate limit raise. This works fine.

1NT Semi-Forcing is definitely a convention that merits your consideration. In fact, when the 1NT bidder is a passed hand, everyone who plays 1NT Forcing should treat 1NT as Semi-Forcing.

Nicely Done

Contract: 4♡
Lead: ♡2

North
♠ A J 7 5 4 3
♡ A 10
♢ 2
♣ A K 9 8

West
♠ K 10 9 8
♡ 7 4 2
♢ A 10 8
♣ 7 4 3

East
♠ Q 6
♡ J 5
♢ K J 7 5 4
♣ Q J 10 6

South
♠ 2
♡ K Q 9 8 6 3
♢ Q 9 6 3
♣ 5 2

South	West	North	East
—	Pass	1♠	Pass
1NT	Pass	2♣	Pass
2♡	Pass	4♡	All Pass

North's economical 2♣ bid was the key. When South showed long hearts, North knew that 4♡ had to have play. Because North had to be short in diamonds, West led a trump. This prevented declarer from using dummy's short suit, so he planned to go to work on North's long suit.

South won the trump lead with his ♡K, and led a spade to dummy's ace and ruffed a spade. Declarer led a heart to the ♡A and ruffed another spade. South pulled West's last trump and led a club to the board. A third spade ruff extinguished West's ♠K. South led a club to dummy's ♣K, and cashed two spade tricks. Making five.

Finding Hearts After Spades

After a spade bid, finding a heart fit can be difficult. This is especially true when playing 1NT Forcing. If partner opens 1♠, responder is not strong enough to respond 2♡, even if he had 11 HCP, such as:

♠ J   ♡ Q J 8 6 2   ◇ 8 7 2   ♣ A K 5 3

In addition, when the auction proceeds: 1♠ – 1NT
                                          2◇ – ???

Responder still shouldn't bid 2♡ — that shows a 6-card suit and a weak hand. The result of all these constraints is that responder is never "allowed" to bid his 5-card major. If opener has three hearts, the 5-3 fit may be gone forever.

However, there is a solution. If opener has three hearts AND is strong enough to bid again, he should bid hearts at his third turn. For example:

West	*West*	*East*	*East*
♠ A 8 7 4 3	1♠	1NT	♠ J
♡ A 10 7	2◇	2NT	♡ Q J 8 6 2
◇ A K 6 3	3♡	4♡	◇ 8 7 2
♣ 4	Pass		♣ A K 5 3

By the way: After   1♠ – 1NT
                         2♣ – ???

Some experienced players use an artificial 2◇ bid (called "Bart") to look for a possible 5-3 heart fit. However, Bart is NOT an easy-to-use convention.

Other Responses of 1NT to a Major
(None of these 1NT bids are forcing)

1NT Response by a Passed Hand:
(Logically Semi-Forcing)

- 5-11 HCP
- Balanced or unbalanced
- Can still have a very weak 3-card raise
- With a 3-card limit raise, I strongly recommend playing Reverse Drury (bid 2♣).

1NT after Partner Opens 1♡ and RHO Overcalls 1♠:
(Passed hand or unpassed hand)

- 7-10 HCP
- Guarantees a stopper in RHO's spade suit
- No singleton or void
- Denies 3-card heart support

1NT Response after RHO Doubles:
(Passed hand or unpassed hand)

- 7-9 HCP (redouble with 10)
- No singleton or void
- Denies 3-card support

Opponent Interferes, After a 1NT Response

After an opponent overcalls (or doubles), the player who responded 1NT will get a chance to bid again. Therefore, as opener, you're free to pass and are not required to bid a 3-card minor. But suppose opener doesn't want to pass:

After RHO Overcalls (or weak jump-overcalls)

Double – In "Standard," opener's double is for penalties. At the two level, I strongly prefer to play double as takeout (alertable), which saves room and preserves all options. Opener can have a shapely minimum, or a good hand, or even a great hand. If RHO jump-overcalls, a double shows "cards" — a strong hand which has no convenient bid.

Bid – If opener bids, he doesn't promise extra values, but he does need a reason.

Cue-Bid – Forcing to game. Any shape is possible.

After RHO Doubles (for takeout)

Redouble promises extra values (at least 15 HCP) and forces opener's side to compete further. Jumps emphasize shape, as opposed to HCP.

By the way:

South	West	North	East
1♠	Pass	1NT	2♡
Pass	Pass	???	

Most, but not all, players treat responder's double as penalty, and 2NT as natural and invitational. As always, the partnership must be on the same wavelength.

Examples of Coping with Interference

What Should Opener Do?

South	West	North	East
1♡	Pass	1NT	2♠
???			

♠ 8 ♡ A K 8 6 5 ◇ J 7 5 3 ♣ A K 9

Double (alertable) is perfect if your partnership treats it as a takeout double. If you treat a double as penalty (Standard), I suppose you would bid 3 ◇ (Yuck).

♠ J 7 6 ♡ K J 6 5 3 2 ◇ Q 9 ♣ A K

Pass. In order to rebid 3♡, you need either a better hand or a better suit.

South	West	North	East
1♠	Pass	1NT	Dbl
???			

♠ A J 10 7 5 3 ♡ K 5 2 ◇ A 4 ♣ A 3

Redouble. You *were* planning to jump to 3♠, but East's double allows you to do even better. Redouble followed by 2♠ describes this hand while remaining at the two level. In addition, once your opponents retreat, partner may be able to double for penalties.

♠ K Q 10 6 2 ♡ — ◇ A Q 7 6 4 2 ♣ 7 4

Jump to 3◇, promising GREAT shape, without a lot of HCP. If you had enough HCP to jump-shift, you would have redoubled.

Responder's Impossible Spade Rebid
(After 1♡ - 1NT)

A 1NT response (to 1♡) denies four spades. If responder later follows with a spade bid, it *must* be artificial.

If opener rebids 2♣, 2♢, or 2♡, responder's 2♠ rebid:
Shows more HCP than if he went directly to the three level, and is alertable. Opener must now bid 2NT (also alertable), and responder will bid the appropriate minor suit.

$$1♡ - 1NT$$
$$2♢ - ???$$

Bid 3♣, obviously, with:
♠ 6 2 ♡ 6 4 ♢ K 9 ♣ Q J 9 8 5 4 2

Bid 2♠, then 3♣, with:
♠ 6 2 ♡ 6 4 ♢ A 9 6 ♣ K Q J 9 8 5

Bid 3♢, obviously, with:
♠ A 8 5 ♡ 7 ♢ K 9 7 6 4 ♣ J 6 5 2

Bid 2♠, then 3♢, with:
♠ A 8 5 ♡ 7 ♢ A Q 9 7 6 ♣ J 6 5 2

Impossible 3♠ Rebid: If opener jumps after 1♡ – 1NT, responder can rebid 3♠ (alertable) to say that he does not know what to do. This flexible bid preserves all options.

$$1♡ - 1NT$$
$$3♡ - ???$$

♠ 7 5 4 ♡ 2 ♢ A K Q 10 ♣ Q 6 5 3 2
Bid 3♠. Without the Impossible 3♠ Rebid, good luck!

1NT Forcing Issues to Resolve

Every partnership is more effective when both players are on the same page. Make sure you reach an agreement on each of these topics.

When partner opens a major:

1. Is 1NT forcing, or is it only semi-forcing?
2. Is 1NT forcing by a passed hand?
3. Do you play 2/1 Game-Forcing, so that responder's new suit at the two level is 100% game-forcing?

4. Is a new suit by responder forcing to game?

a. After 1♡ – 1NT   b. 1♡ or 1♠ – 1NT
       2♠ – ???   2NT – ???

5. In example 4b, how many HCP does 2NT show?
6. If opener jumps to the three level, is responder's new suit (nonjump) at the four level natural?

Responder's Impossible Spade Rebids
(after auction begins 1♡ - 1NT)

7. If responder's next bid is 2♠, what does it indicate?
8. If opener jumps, what does 3♠ indicate?

Competitive Doubles:

9. By opener at the two level — takeout or penalty?
10. By opener at the three level — "cards" or penalty?
11. By responder — penalty, "cards," or takeout?

When Your RHO Bids 1NT Forcing

If you pass, you'll still get a second chance, and can decide to balance later on. However, that does not mean you should automatically pass now and think later. **If you have an appropriate action, there's no time like the present.**

After 1♡ – Pass – 1NT – ???

Double = takeout of opener's suit. Because you are forcing a potentially broke partner to bid at the two level, you need excellent shape or a fistful of HCP.

2♣, 2♢, 2♠ = normal overcalls. Usually a 6-card suit.

2♡ = Michaels Cue-Bid. Promises five spades and at least five cards in an unspecified minor suit. If partner needs to know your minor, he will respond 2NT.

2NT = Unusual Notrump, at least five cards in each minor.

Jump-overcall = Preemptive. At least a 6-card suit.
Suit length and strength are based on the vulnerability.

Opening Lead Advice:

After your opponents bid:

    1 of a major – 1NT
    2 of a minor – Pass

Lead a trump, almost without looking at your hand!

46

Hardcover Books by Marty Bergen

More Declarer Play the Bergen Way	$18.95
Declarer Play the Bergen Way	**$18.95**
Bergen for the Defense	$18.95
MARTY SEZ... Volumes 1, 2 & 3	$17.95 *each*
****POINTS SCHMOINTS!***	**$19.95**
More POINTS SCHMOINTS!	$19.95
Better Bidding with Bergen, Vol. 1	$16.95
Better Bidding with Bergen, Vol. 2	$14.95

*Winners of the award as "Bridge Book of the Year"

Softcover Books by Marty Bergen
Buy 2, then get 1 (equal or lesser price) for half price!

Bergen's Best Bridge Tips	$7.95
Bergen's Best Bridge Quizzes, Vol. 1	$7.95
To Open or Not to Open	$6.95
Better Rebidding with Bergen	$7.95
Understanding 1NT Forcing	$5.95
Hand Evaluation: Points, Schmoints!	$7.95
Introduction to Negative Doubles	$6.95
Negative Doubles	$9.95

•• VERY SPECIAL OFFER ••

Buy one hardcover book from Marty and receive a **free** copy
of any one of his eight softcover books.
Buy 2 hardcovers and get 3 free softcover books!
Personalized autographs available upon request.

The Official Encyclopedia of Bridge (more than 800 pages)

Highlights include extensive sections on: suit combinations,
explanation of all conventions, techniques for bidding, defense,
leads, declarer play, and a complete glossary of bridge terms.
The encyclopedia sells for $39.95. Marty's special offer:
Pay only $23 and also get a free softcover book!

Interactive CDs for the Computer

Guaranteed to improve your game. Great graphics!

by Marty Bergen

POINTS SCHMOINTS!	~~$29.95~~	$25
Marty Sez...	~~$24.95~~	$20

Very Special Offer! Get both CDs for $30
For free demos of Bergen CDs, e-mail Marty at:
mbergen@mindspring.com
Mention this book and get a free Bergen softcover
(choice of 8) with each Lawrence or Gitelman CD!

Five CDs by Mike Lawrence

Conventions, Defense, 2/1, Private Lessons 1 and 2 (declarer play). Marty's discount price is $30 each (*Conventions* is $35).

by Fred Gitelman

Bridge Master 2000   ~~$59.95~~ $48
"Best software ever created for improving your declarer play."

Cavendish 2000 by Kit Woolsey

Day 1, Days 2-3   ~~$29.95~~ $19 each

Play Bridge with Larry Cohen (Special Sale)

Free demos available at: larryco.com/index.html

Day 1, Day 2, Day 3	~~$29.95~~	$19 each
My Favorite 52	~~$29.95~~	$19

Day 1 and *My Favorite 52* won awards for best software

• ORDERING INFORMATION •

Call Marty toll-free: **1-800-386-7432.** All major credit cards accepted. Checks and money orders in U.S. funds also okay.

Marty Bergen
9 River Chase Terrace
Palm Beach Gardens, FL 33418
If ordering by mail, please call or email for S&H details.